It's All About Zucchini
50 Fabulous Recipes

DAHLIA ORION

Copyright © 2019 Dahlia Orion. All rights reserved.

ISBN-13: 9781098600761

Table of Contents

Banana-Zucchini Bread 7
Bayou Shrimp Creole Bake 8
Bubbly Zucchini & Cheese 9
Burgers with Chunky Grilled Vegetables 10
California Grilled Veggie Sandwich 11
Cheesy Vegetable Lasagna 12
Cheesy Zucchini Casserole 13
Garden Paella 14
Choco-Zucchini Muffins 15
Cinderella Pumpkin Bowl with Vegetables 16
Colorful Carnival Chopped Salad 17
Colorful Zucchini Spears 18
Deepest Desire Zucchini Cake 19
Delicious Barley Bake 20
Easy Tortellini Soup 22
Eggplant & Zucchini Casserole 23
Garden Penne 24
Greek Goddess Pasta Salad 25
Grilled Garlic Parmesan Zucchini 26
Grilled Greek-Style Zucchini 27
Honey Rosemary Chicken Kabobs 28
Italian Lamb Stew 29
Italian Ribollita (Vegetable and Bread Soup) 30
Jolly Green Giant Chicken 31
Lemon Orzo Primavera 32
Marrakesh Vegetable Curry 33
Mediterranean Yellow Rice & Vegetables 34
Mighty Delish Moroccan Chicken 35
Mouthwatering Meatless Lasagna 36
Over The Rainbow Veggie Chili 38
Presidential Pistou Soup 39
Prosciutto-Wrapped Chicken with Mediterranean Veggies
.... 40
Rice with Summer Squash 41
Saucy Beef and Vegetable Casserole 42
Sesame Zucchini Bread 43
Spring Vegetable Medley 44
Stuffed Peppers with Turkey & Vegetables 45
Summer Bliss Veggie Casserole 46
Super Summer Garden Pork Chops 47

Vegetarian Lasagna... 48
Veggie Shrimp Fettuccine 49
Veggie Stir-Fry 49
Zesty Zucchini with Salsa 50
Zucchilattas... 51
Zucchini Cobbler 52
Zucchini Cocoa Cupcakes... 53
Zucchini Cream Pie.. 54
Zucchini Pineapple Bread 55
Zucchini Walnut Bread 56
Zucchini-Coconut Cookie Bars.. 57
Zucchini-Potato Soup 58

"When I pass a flowering zucchini plant in a garden, my heart skips a beat." -*Gwyneth Paltrow*

Zucchini are healthy and delicious botanical fruits (though typically thought of and treated as a vegetable) offering extremely high nutritional value and extremely low calorie counts, making them great options for dieters and those looking to increase their fiber intake. Zucchini can be easily grown at home or sourced at the local grocery store or famer's market, and can be found year-round. They are at their best during the late spring and summer seasons. The health benefits of zucchini include:

- High antioxidant value; used by many nutritionists for weight reduction and cholesterol control programs by the dieticians.
- Excellent source of the heart friendly electrolyte potassium, which means zucchini can help reduce blood pressure and heart rates by countering the pressure effects of sodium.
- High levels of the B-complex group of vitamins like thiamine, pyridoxine, riboflavin and minerals like iron, manganese, phosphorus, and zinc.

Preparation Tips:

Zucchini are easy to cook. A good cold water wash prior to cooking is always in order along with a light scrub to remove prickles and clumps of dirt. Zucchini skins are highly nutritious and really should not be removed. For those who choose to grow their own, zucchini blossoms are also an edible delicacy, best picked during morning hours when they are fresh and soft. To prepare, open up blossoms and carefully check for insects and rinse well.

- Fresh, tender zucchini can be eaten raw in salads.
- Zucchini pods can be fried, boiled, baked, or steamed, and seasoned in myriad ways.

- Zucchini are great in veggie medleys alongside potatoes, carrots, asparagus, or green beans.
- Zucchini can be chopped or grated into breads, pizza dough, and other baked goods for additional flavor and nutrition.

Banana-Zucchini Bread

Ingredients

3 eggs
3/4 cup vegetable oil
2/3 cup packed brown sugar
1 cup white sugar
1 cup grated zucchini
2 bananas, mashed
2 teaspoons vanilla extract
3 1/2 cups all-purpose flour
1 tablespoon ground cinnamon
1 1/2 teaspoons baking powder
1 teaspoon baking soda
1 teaspoon salt
1/2 cup dried cranberries
1/2 cup chopped walnuts

Directions

Preheat oven to 325 degrees F (165 degrees C). Grease and flour two 8x4 inch bread loaf pans. In a large bowl, beat eggs until light yellow and frothy. Add oil, brown sugar, white sugar, grated zucchini, bananas, and vanilla; blend together until well combined. Stir in the flour, cinnamon, baking powder, baking soda, and salt. Mix in the cranberries and nuts. Divide the batter evenly between the two prepared loaf pans. Bake in the preheated oven until a toothpick inserted in the center comes out clean, about 50 minutes. Allow to cool in the loaf pans on a wire rack before removing and serving.

Bayou Shrimp Creole Bake

<u>Ingredients</u>

2 cups water
1 1/4 cups uncooked white rice
2 onions, diced
2 cups sliced mushrooms
5 carrots, sliced
1 green bell pepper, diced
1 1/2 cups diced celery
1 zucchini, sliced
1 (15 ounce) can seasoned tomato sauce
1 (16 ounce) can whole peeled tomatoes, crushed
2 tablespoons butter
1 (4 ounce) jar chopped pimento peppers
1 1/2 pounds cooked medium shrimp, peeled and deveined
2 teaspoons chili powder

<u>Directions</u>

In a saucepan bring salted water to a boil. Add rice, reduce heat, cover and simmer for 20 minutes. Preheat oven to 350 degrees F (175 degrees C). Sauté the mushrooms, carrots, onions, green pepper, celery, and zucchini in butter until tender. Add all the tomatoes, tomato sauce, pimientos, and shrimp. Stir in rice and chili powder. Pour mixture into a 9x13 inch casserole dish. Bake at 350 degrees F (175 degrees C) for 1 hour.

Bubbly Zucchini & Cheese

<u>Ingredients</u>

2 tablespoons unsalted butter
1 large zucchini, chopped
1 large white onion, chopped
4 tomatoes, chopped
1 large green bell pepper, chopped dried
Italian seasoning to taste
1 (8 ounce) package shredded mozzarella cheese

<u>Directions</u>

Preheat oven to 350 degrees F (175 degrees C). Lightly grease a medium casserole dish. Melt the butter in a skillet over medium heat. Stir in the zucchini and onion, and cook 5 minutes, or until onion is golden brown. In the prepared casserole dish, mix the zucchini, onion, tomatoes, and green pepper. Season with Italian seasoning, and top with cheese. Bake 25 minutes in the preheated oven, or until cheese is melted and bubbly.

Burgers with Chunky Grilled Vegetables

Ingredients

1/3 cup balsamic vinegar
2 teaspoons olive oil
1 teaspoon minced garlic
1/2 medium yellow bell pepper
1/2 medium red bell pepper
1 small zucchini, halved lengthwise
1 baby eggplant or Japanese eggplant, halved lengthwise
4 burger patties of your choice

Directions

In small saucepan cook vinegar over low heat about 5 minutes or until reduced to 2 tablespoons and syrupy. Set aside. in small bowl stir together olive oil and garlic. Brush bell peppers, Zucchini and eggplant with olive oil mixture. Grill peppers and zucchini over medium heat for 5 minutes, turning occasionally. Add burgers and eggplant to grill. Grill for 4 to 6 minutes more or until burgers are heated through and vegetables are tender, turning occasionally. Remove from grill. Cut vegetables into 3/4- to 1-inch pieces. To serve, spoon vegetables on burgers. Drizzle with balsamic vinegar.

California Grilled Veggie Sandwich

<u>Ingredients</u>

1/4 cup mayonnaise
3 cloves garlic, minced
1 tablespoon lemon juice
1/8 cup olive oil
1 cup sliced red bell peppers
1 small zucchini, sliced
1 red onion, sliced
1 small yellow squash, sliced
2 (4-x6-inch) focaccia bread pieces, split horizontally
1/2 cup crumbled feta cheese

<u>Directions</u>

In a bowl, mix the mayonnaise, minced garlic, and lemon juice. Set aside in the refrigerator. Preheat the grill for high heat. Brush vegetables with olive oil on each side. Brush grate with oil. Place bell peppers and zucchini closest to the middle of the grill, and set onion and squash pieces around them. Cook for about 3 minutes, turn, and cook for another 3 minutes. The peppers may take a bit longer. Remove from grill, and set aside. Spread some of the mayonnaise mixture on the cut sides of the bread, and sprinkle each one with feta cheese. Place on the grill cheese side up, and cover with lid for 2 to 3 minutes. This will warm the bread, and slightly melt the cheese. Watch carefully so the bottoms don't burn. Remove from grill, and layer with the vegetables. Enjoy as open faced grilled sandwiches.

Cheesy Vegetable Lasagna

Ingredients

1 (10 ounce) package frozen chopped spinach, thawed
1 (8 ounce) container small curd cottage cheese
1 large onion, chopped
1/2 cup all-purpose flour
1/2 teaspoon pepper
1/2 teaspoon salt
12 lasagna noodles
2 1/2 cups shredded mozzarella cheese, divided
2 carrots, thinly sliced
2 green bell peppers, chopped
2 heads fresh broccoli, chopped
2 small zucchinis, sliced
2 tablespoons olive oil
24 ounces ricotta cheese
3 cloves garlic, minced
3 cups milk
3/4 cup Parmesan cheese, divided

Directions

Preheat oven to 375 degrees F (190 degrees C). Grease a 9 x 13-inch casserole dish. Bring a large pot of lightly salted water to a boil. Add lasagna noodles and cook for 8 to 10 minutes or until al dente; drain. Heat oil in a large cast iron skillet over medium heat. When oil is hot add broccoli, carrots, onions, bell peppers, zucchini and garlic. Sauté for 7 minutes; set aside. Place flour in a medium saucepan and gradually whisk in milk until well blended. Bring to a boil over medium heat. Cook 5 minutes, or until thick, stirring constantly. Stir in 1/2 cup Parmesan cheese, salt and pepper; cook for 1 minute, stirring constantly. Remove from heat; stir in spinach. Reserve 1/2 cup spinach mixture. In a small bowl combine cottage and ricotta cheeses; stir well. Spread about 1/2 cup of spinach mixture in the bottom of the prepared pan. Layer noodles, ricotta mixture, vegetables, spinach mixture and 2 cups mozzarella cheese, ending with noodles. Top with reserved spinach mixture, 1/2 cup mozzarella cheese and 1/4 cup parmesan cheese. Bake in preheated oven for 35 minutes, or until lightly browned on top. Cool for approximately 10 minutes before serving.

Cheesy Zucchini Casserole

Ingredients
9 zucchinis, peeled and sliced
1 large onion, chopped
1/2 cup butter
1 1/2 cups shredded Cheddar cheese
3 eggs, beaten
Salt and pepper to taste
48 buttery round crackers, crushed

Directions
Preheat oven to 350 degrees F (175 degrees C). Grease a 2-quart casserole dish. Boil zucchini and onion in a large pot for about 10 minutes; drain. To the zucchini and onion add the butter, cheese, eggs, salt and pepper. Transfer to prepared baking dish and sprinkle cracker crumbs on top. Bake in preheated oven for 1 hour.

Garden Paella

Ingredients
1 large onion, chopped
2 tablespoons olive or canola oil
1 1/2 cups uncooked long grain rice
3 garlic cloves, minced
2 1/2 cups vegetable broth
1 1/2 cups sliced carrots
1 1/2 cups frozen cut green beans, thawed
1 medium sweet red pepper, julienned
1 medium zucchini, quartered lengthwise and cut into 1/2 inch slices
1 teaspoon salt
1/2 teaspoon dried thyme
1/4 teaspoon ground turmeric
1/8 teaspoon paprika
1 (14 ounce) can water-packed artichoke hearts, drained and quartered
2 plum tomatoes, seeded and chopped
1 cup frozen peas, thawed
1 cup frozen corn, thawed

Directions
In a large nonstick skillet, sauté onion in oil for 2 minutes. Add rice and garlic; sauté 1 minute longer. Add the next nine ingredients; mix well. Bring to a boil. Reduce heat; cover and simmer for 25-30 minutes or until liquid is absorbed and rice is tender. Stir in the artichoke hearts, tomatoes, peas and corn; heat through.

Choco-Zucchini Muffins

<u>Ingredients</u>

3 eggs
2 cups white sugar
1 cup vegetable oil
1/3 cup unsweetened cocoa powder
1 1/2 teaspoons vanilla extract
2 cups grated zucchini
3 cups all-purpose flour
1 teaspoon baking soda
1/2 teaspoon baking powder
1 teaspoon salt
1/4 teaspoon ground cinnamon
1/4 teaspoon ground nutmeg
1/4 teaspoon ground cloves
1/4 teaspoon ground cardamom

<u>Directions</u>

Preheat oven to 350 degrees F (175 degrees C). Lightly grease or line two 12 cup muffin tins with paper liners. In a large bowl beat the eggs. Beat in the sugar and oil. Add the cocoa, vanilla, zucchini and stir well. Stir in the flour, baking soda, baking powder, salt, cinnamon, nutmeg, cloves and cardamom. Mix until just moist. Pour batter into prepared muffin tins filling 2/3 of the way full. Bake at 350 degrees F (175 degrees C) for 20 to 25 minutes. Remove from pan and let cool on a wire rack. Store loosely covered.

Cinderella Pumpkin Bowl with Vegetables

Ingredients

1 whole (10 pound) Cinderella pumpkin
1 (16 ounce) package kielbasa sausage, sliced into 1/2 inch pieces
3 carrots, peeled and sliced
2 celery ribs, chopped
1 large onion, peeled and chopped
3 cloves garlic - minced, or amount to taste
2 cups parsnips, peeled and cubed (optional)
2 cups rutabagas, peeled and cubed (optional)
2 cups cabbage, coarsely chopped (optional)
1 green bell pepper, chopped
1 red bell pepper, chopped
1 head broccoli, cut into florets
2 zucchinis, cut into chunks
1 1/2 cups canned or frozen corn
2 (13.75 ounce) cans chicken broth
2 cups cooked white or brown rice (optional)
1/2 cup chopped fresh parsley
1/2 teaspoon red pepper flakes, or to taste
1/2 (1.25 ounce) envelope dry onion soup mix
1/2 (1 ounce) packet dried Italian seasoning
Salt and ground black pepper to taste

Directions

Preheat oven to 400 degrees F (200 degrees C). Line a baking sheet with foil. Cut around the top of the pumpkin to make a lid. Use a large metal spoon to scoop out the inside membrane and seeds. Place the pumpkin on the prepared baking sheet, and place in the preheated oven. Cook for 1 hour, then lower heat to 325 degrees F (165 degrees C). Meanwhile, place the sausage in a deep pot over medium-high heat. Cook until evenly browned, turning frequently, 10 to 12 minutes. Stir in the carrots, celery, onion, and garlic; cook and stir until translucent and tender, about 5 minutes. If desired, stir in the parsnips, rutabaga, and/or the cabbage; cook until the vegetables are almost tender, about 5 minutes. Add the red and green peppers, broccoli, zucchini, and corn. Pour in the chicken broth, add the rice, and cook 5 minutes more. Stir in the parsley, red pepper flakes, onion soup mix, and Italian seasoning. Season to taste with salt and pepper. Keeping the pumpkin on the baking sheet, spoon the vegetable- sausage mixture into the pumpkin, and replace the lid. Loosely cover the pumpkin with aluminum foil. Cook the pumpkin in the preheated oven until the flesh is tender, about 4 hours. Scoop some of the pumpkin flesh away from the sides to combine with the vegetable mixture. To serve, place the pumpkin on a serving platter, and remove the lid to ladle out the contents.

Colorful Carnival Chopped Salad

Ingredients
1 medium sweet red pepper, chopped
1 medium sweet yellow pepper, chopped
1 medium tomato, seeded and chopped
1 medium cucumber, seeded and chopped
1 small zucchini, chopped
2 green onions, chopped
2 tablespoons minced fresh parsley

2 tablespoons olive oil
1 tablespoon red wine vinegar
1/2 teaspoon sugar
1/4 teaspoon salt
1/4 teaspoon pepper
1 large ripe avocado, peeled and chopped
1 tablespoon lemon juice

Directions

In a large bowl, combine the first seven ingredients. In a jar with a tight-fitting lid, combine the oil, vinegar, sugar, salt and pepper; shake well. Drizzle over vegetables and toss to coat. Toss avocado with lemon juice; sprinkle over salad. Serve with a slotted spoon.

Colorful Zucchini Spears

Ingredients

1 slice bacon, cut into 1 inch pieces
1 medium zucchini
1/8 teaspoon salt
1/8 teaspoon dried oregano
1/8 teaspoon garlic powder
1/8 teaspoon pepper
1 plum tomato, halved and sliced
1/4 cup sliced onion
1/4 cup shredded reduced-fat sharp Cheddar cheese

Directions

In a small nonstick skillet, cook bacon over medium heat until cooked but not crisp. Using a slotted spoon, remove bacon to paper towels to drain. Cut zucchini in half widthwise; cut halves lengthwise into quarters. Place in an ungreased shallow 1-qt. baking dish.

Combine the salt, oregano, garlic powder and pepper; sprinkle half over the zucchini. Top with tomato, onion, remaining seasonings and bacon. Bake, uncovered, at 350 degrees F for 15 minutes. Sprinkle with cheese; bake 5-10 minutes longer or until zucchini is tender.

Deepest Desire Zucchini Cake

Ingredients
2 eggs
1/4 cup vegetable oil
3/4 cup applesauce
1 1/2 cups brown sugar
2 teaspoons vanilla extract
3 1/2 cups shredded zucchini
1 tablespoon molasses
1 tablespoon honey
4 cups all-purpose flour
1 teaspoon baking soda
1/4 teaspoon baking powder
2 1/4 teaspoons ground cinnamon
3/4 cup chopped pecans (optional)
Directions
Preheat oven to 350 degrees F (175 degrees C). Grease two 8x4 inch loaf pans. In a medium bowl, beat together the eggs with the oil. Stir in the applesauce, brown sugar, vanilla, molasses, and honey. Combine the flour, baking soda, baking powder, and cinnamon; combine with applesauce mixture until just moistened. Finally, stir in the zucchini and nuts. Divide the batter evenly between the prepared pans. Bake for 1 hour in

preheated oven, or until a toothpick inserted comes out clean. Cool in the pan for 15 minutes before removing to a wire rack to cool completely.

Delicious Barley Bake

<u>Ingredients</u>
2 cups barley
4 cups chicken broth
2 tablespoons olive oil
1 cup chopped celery
1 cup chopped carrots
6 cloves garlic, minced
1 cup chopped onion
2 cups sliced mushrooms
1 yellow zucchini, cut into half moons
1 cup fresh green beans, trimmed and cut into 1 inch pieces
2 cups broccoli florets
1 (4 ounce) package cream cheese, softened
1 (10.75 ounce) can condensed cream of chicken soup
1/3 cup sour cream
1/4 cup grated Locatella cheese
1/4 cup grated Parmesan cheese
1 tablespoon garlic powder
1/2 teaspoon ground nutmeg
1 tablespoon dried oregano
1 tablespoon dried basil
1 tablespoon ground thyme
1 cup green peas
1 cup whole kernel corn
1 cup roasted red peppers, drained and chopped

1 (10 ounce) package frozen chopped spinach, thawed and drained
2 cups shredded cooked chicken
salt and ground black pepper to taste
2 cups shredded mozzarella cheese

Directions

Preheat an oven to 350 degrees F (175 degrees C). Bring the barley and chicken broth to a boil in a saucepan over high heat. Cover, reduce heat to low, and simmer until the barley is tender, about 30 minutes. Heat the olive oil in a skillet over medium heat. Stir in the celery, carrots, garlic, and onion; cook and stir until the onion has softened and turned translucent, about 5 minutes. Stir in the mushrooms, zucchini, green beans, and broccoli. Continue cooking and stirring until the broccoli is tender, about 5 minutes more. Remove skillet from heat. Combine cream cheese, cream of chicken soup, sour cream, Locatella cheese, Parmesan cheese, garlic powder, nutmeg, oregano, basil, and thyme in a large bowl, mixing until smooth. Stir in the prepared barley, peas, corn, roasted red peppers, spinach, and shredded chicken. Season with salt and pepper. Spread mixture into a large baking dish and top with mozzarella cheese. Bake in the preheated oven until bubbly, and cheese has melted, 20 to 30 minutes.

Easy Tortellini Soup

<u>Ingredients</u>
1 tablespoon olive oil
1 small red onion, chopped
1 zucchini, chopped
1 tablespoon minced garlic
1 (28 ounce) can crushed tomatoes
2 (14.5 ounce) cans chicken broth
1 tablespoon white sugar
1 tablespoon Italian seasoning
1/4 cup red wine
1 dash hot pepper sauce
1 (11 ounce) can white corn, undrained
1/2 cup freshly grated Parmesan cheese
8 ounces cheese tortellini

<u>Directions</u>
In a large pot over medium heat, cook onion, zucchini and garlic in oil three minutes, until onion is translucent. Stir in crushed tomatoes, broth, sugar, Italian seasoning, wine and pepper sauce and bring to a boil. Reduce heat and stir in corn and Parmesan. Simmer 30 minutes. Stir in tortellini and simmer 10 minutes more, until pasta is tender.

Eggplant & Zucchini Casserole

Ingredients

2 cups water
4 tablespoons butter
8 ounces dry bread stuffing mix
1 large eggplant, diced
2 large zucchinis, diced
1 onion, chopped
1 tomato, chopped
1 teaspoon dried thyme
2 cups shredded Colby cheese
salt to taste ground black pepper to taste

Directions

In a microwavable bowl, mix water and margarine (cut into pieces). Stir in stuffing mix and cover with a microwavable lid. Cook on HIGH for 8 to 10 minutes. Fluff with fork. Place eggplant, zucchini, tomato, onion into a large skillet. Season with thyme, salt, and pepper. Cook and stir over medium low heat for 15 to 20 minutes. Remove from heat. Preheat oven to 350 degrees F (175 degrees C). Grease a 2-quart casserole dish. Layer vegetables, cheese, and stuffing in the dish until all Ingredients have been used, ending with cheese. Bake for 30 to 40 minutes.

Garden Penne

Ingredients
1 (16 ounce) package penne pasta
1 tablespoon olive oil
2 zucchinis, chopped
2 yellow squash, chopped
1 red onion, chopped
1 red bell pepper, chopped
1 green bell pepper, chopped
1 tablespoon crushed garlic
1 (28 ounce) can diced tomatoes, drained
1 (28 ounce) jar chunky style pasta sauce
1 (15.25 ounce) can whole kernel corn, drained
1 teaspoon crushed red pepper, or to taste
1/2 teaspoon black pepper, or to taste
2 cups shredded mozzarella cheese

Directions
Fill a large pot with lightly salted water and bring to a rolling boil over high heat. Once the water is boiling, stir in the penne, and return to a boil. Cook the pasta uncovered, stirring occasionally, until the pasta has cooked through, but is still firm to the bite, about 11 minutes. Drain well in a colander set in the sink, place the pasta in a large bowl, and set aside. While the pasta is cooking, heat the oil in a large skillet over medium heat, and cook and stir the zucchini, squash, onion, red and green peppers, and garlic until the vegetables are tender, for about 10 minutes. Pour in the tomatoes, pasta sauce, and corn, and stir to mix. Sprinkle with red and black pepper to taste, and bring the mixture back to a boil. Simmer for 20 minutes.

Preheat an oven to 350 degrees F (175 degrees C). Grease a 9x13 inch baking dish. Pour the vegetable mixture into the bowl with the cooked penne pasta, stir to mix well, and spoon into the prepared baking dish. Sprinkle the mozzarella cheese over the top, and bake in the preheated oven until the cheese is melted and the casserole is bubbling, 20 to 30 minutes.

Greek Goddess Pasta Salad

Ingredients
1 (12 ounce) package tri-colored rotini pasta
1 small head broccoli, broken into small florets
1/2 teaspoon minced garlic
1 small red onion, diced
1 (12 ounce) jar marinated artichoke hearts, drained and chopped
1 (12 ounce) jar pitted Kalamata olives, sliced
1 (8 ounce) jar roasted red bell peppers, drained, cut into strips
4 Roma tomatoes, diced
1 (12 ounce) jar oil-packed sun- dried tomatoes, drained, cut into strips
1 small zucchini, chopped
1 small cucumber, chopped
1 small yellow bell pepper, chopped
2 ripe avocados
1 (16 ounce) bottle Greek vinaigrette salad dressing
Directions
Fill a large pot with lightly salted water and bring to a rolling boil over high heat. Once the water is boiling,

stir in the pasta, and return to a boil. Cook the pasta uncovered, stirring occasionally, until the pasta has cooked through, but is still firm to the bite, about 10 minutes. Drain well in a colander set in the sink, rinse with cool water and place in a large bowl. Place a steamer insert into a saucepan, and fill with water to just below the bottom of the steamer. Cover, and bring the water to a boil over high heat. Add the broccoli, recover, and steam until just tender, 2 to 6 minutes depending on thickness. Rinse the broccoli with cold water, finely chop, and add to pasta. Stir in the garlic, red onion, artichoke hearts, Kalamata olives, roasted red peppers, Roma tomatoes, sun—dried tomatoes, zucchini, cucumber, and yellow pepper and combine well. Cut the avocados in half, remove the pit, and remove from the skin with a large spoon. Cut the avocados into large pieces, place in a small bowl and mash well with a fork. Slowly whisk in the Greek dressing until well combined. Pour the Greek-avocado dressing into the pasta salad and gently toss. Refrigerate for at least one hour before serving.

Grilled Garlic Parmesan Zucchini

Ingredients
3 zucchini
3 tablespoons butter, softened
2 cloves garlic, minced
1 tablespoon chopped fresh parsley
1/2 cup freshly grated Parmesan cheese
Directions
Preheat an outdoor grill for medium-high heat, and

lightly oil the grate. Cut the zucchini in half crosswise, then slice each half into 3 slices lengthwise, making 6 slices per zucchini. Mix the butter, garlic, and parsley in a bowl, and spread the mixture on both sides of each zucchini slice. Sprinkle one side of each slice with Parmesan cheese, and place the slices, cheese sides up, crosswise on the preheated grill to keep them from falling through. Grill the zucchini until the cheese has melted and the slices are cooked through and show grill marks, about 8 minutes.

Grilled Greek-Style Zucchini

Ingredients
4 small zucchinis, thinly sliced
1 medium tomato, seeded and chopped
1/4 cup pitted ripe olives, halved
2 tablespoons chopped green onion
4 teaspoons olive or canola oil
2 teaspoons lemon juice
1/2 teaspoon dried oregano
1/2 teaspoon garlic salt
1/4 teaspoon pepper
2 tablespoons grated Parmesan cheese

Directions
In a bowl, combine the zucchini, tomato, olives and onion. Combine oil, lemon juice, oregano, garlic salt and pepper; pour over vegetables and toss to coat. Place on a double thickness of heavy- duty foil (about 23 in. x 18 in.). Fold foil around vegetables and seal tightly. Grill, covered, over medium heat for 10-15 minutes or until vegetables are tender. Sprinkle with

Parmesan cheese.

Honey Rosemary Chicken Kabobs

Ingredients
1/3 cup honey
1/4 cup lemon juice
2 tablespoons minced fresh rosemary
1/4 teaspoon crushed red pepper flakes
1-pound boneless skinless chicken breasts, cut into 1-inch cubes
1-pint cherry tomatoes
1 small zucchini, cut into 1-inch pieces
1 (8 ounce) can unsweetened pineapple chunks, drained

Directions
In a bowl, combine the first four ingredients. Pour 1/3 cup marinade into a large resealable plastic bag; add the chicken. Seal bag and turn to coat; refrigerate for at least 30 minutes. Cover and refrigerate remaining marinade. Coat grill rack with nonstick cooking spray before starting the grill. Drain and discard marinade from chicken. On eight metal or soaked wooden skewers, alternately thread chicken, vegetables and pineapple. Grill kabobs, covered, over low heat for 9-11 minutes or until chicken juices run clear, turning and basting frequently with reserved marinade.

Italian Lamb Stew

<u>Ingredients</u>

2 tablespoons olive oil
1 1/2 pounds boneless lamb shoulder, cut into 1-inch cubes
salt and ground black pepper to taste
5 cloves garlic, sliced thin
1/2 cup red wine
1/2 cup chicken broth
4 cups peeled, chopped tomatoes
1 teaspoon dried oregano
1 bay leaf
4 potatoes, peeled and cut into 1- inch pieces
2 cups fresh green beans, trimmed
1 red bell pepper, seeded and cut into 1-inch pieces
2 small zucchinis, sliced
3 tablespoons chopped fresh parsley

<u>Directions</u>

Heat the olive oil in a Dutch oven or large, heavy-bottomed pot. Season the lamb with salt and pepper; cook in the hot oil until browned, 2 to 3 minutes. Add the garlic; cook and stir 1 minute. Pour the red wine and chicken broth into the pan and bring to a boil while scraping the browned bits of food off of the bottom of the pot with a wooden spoon. Reduce the heat to medium—low; add the tomatoes, oregano, and bay leaf to the pot. Simmer gently until the lamb is tender, about 45 minutes. Raise heat to medium-high. Add the potatoes, green beans, red pepper, and zucchini to the pot. Cook until the vegetables are tender, another 15 to 20 minutes. Sprinkle the parsley over the soup. Remove the bay leaf and season with salt and pepper before serving.

Italian Ribollita (Vegetable and Bread Soup)

Ingredients

1 tablespoon olive oil
1 large red onion, diced
2 carrots, diced
1 stalk celery, diced
4 potatoes, diced
10 (5 inch) zucchini, diced
1 leek, sliced
1-quart hot water
1 bunch Swiss chard, chopped
1 head Savoy cabbage, quartered, cored and shredded
1 bunch kale, shredded
2 (15.5 ounce) cans cannellini beans, drained and rinsed
Salt and ground black pepper to taste
3 tablespoons tomato puree
8 slices day-old bread

Directions

Place the olive oil in a deep pan and heat over medium-high heat. Stir in the onion, and cook until transparent, about 5 minutes. Mix in the carrots, celery, potatoes, zucchini, and leek. Stir and cook 5 minutes more. Pour in the hot water to cover the vegetables. Stir in the Swiss chard, Savoy cabbage, and kale. Cover, reduce heat to medium, and simmer for 1 hour. Place 1 can of beans in a blender or food processor bowl. Blend until smooth. Stir pureed beans into the vegetable mixture along with the second can of beans. Season to taste with salt and pepper Reduce heat to low, and simmer for 20 minutes, stirring occasionally. Stir in the tomato puree. Prepare the soup by layering slices of bread with the vegetable mixture in a casserole or soup dish. Cover, and refrigerate for at least 8 hours, or overnight. To serve the soup, place in a pot, and reheat over medium heat. Serve hot.

Jolly Green Giant Chicken

Ingredients
1/2 cup sesame oil
3 cloves garlic, chopped
1 small red onion, minced
6 skinless, boneless chicken breast halves
1 teaspoon salt, or to taste
1 teaspoon freshly ground black pepper
1/2 cup chopped fresh parsley
2 cups sliced zucchini
1 cup Parmesan cheese

Directions
Pour the sesame oil into a 9x13 inch baking dish, or any dish large enough to hold your chicken in a single layer. Mix in the garlic and red onion. Lay the chicken breast halves in the dish, and turn to coat. Cover and refrigerate for 3 to 4 hours. Preheat the oven to 350 degrees F (175 degrees C). Uncover the chicken in the dish, and top with sliced zucchini. Season with salt and pepper. Bake uncovered for 1 hour and 30 minutes in the preheated oven. Sprinkle the cheese

over the top of the chicken during the last 15 minutes of baking.

Lemon Orzo Primavera

Ingredients

1 tablespoon olive oil
1 cup uncooked orzo pasta
1 clove garlic, crushed
1 medium zucchini, shredded
1 medium carrot, shredded
1 (14 ounce) can vegetable broth
1 lemon, zested
1 tablespoon chopped fresh thyme
1/4 cup grated Parmesan cheese

Directions

Heat the oil in a pot over medium heat. Stir in orzo, and cook 2 minutes, until golden. Stir in garlic, zucchini, and carrot, and cook 2 minutes. Pour in the broth and mix in lemon zest. Bring to a boil. Reduce heat to low and simmer 10 minutes, or until liquid has been absorbed and orzo is tender. Season with thyme and top with Parmesan to serve.

Marrakesh Vegetable Curry

<u>Ingredients</u>

1 sweet potato, peeled and cubed
1 medium eggplant, cubed
1 green bell pepper, chopped
1 red bell pepper, chopped
2 carrots, chopped
1 onion, chopped
6 tablespoons olive oil
3 cloves garlic, minced
1 teaspoon ground turmeric
1 tablespoon curry powder
1 teaspoon ground cinnamon
3/4 tablespoon sea salt
3/4 teaspoon cayenne pepper
1 (15 ounce) can garbanzo beans, drained
1/4 cup blanched almonds
1 zucchini, sliced
2 tablespoons raisins
1 cup orange juice
10 ounces spinach

<u>Directions</u>

In a large Dutch oven place sweet potato, eggplant, peppers, carrots, onion, and three tablespoons oil. Sauté over medium heat for 5 minutes. In a medium saucepan place 3 tablespoons olive oil, garlic, turmeric, curry powder, cinnamon, salt and pepper and sauté over medium heat for 3 minutes. Pour garlic and spice mixture into the Dutch oven with vegetables in it. Add the garbanzo beans, almonds, zucchini, raisins, and orange juice. Simmer 20 minutes, covered. Add spinach to pot and cook for 5 more minutes. Serve!

Mediterranean Yellow Rice & Vegetables

<u>Ingredients</u>
2 cups vegetable broth
2 cups chicken broth
1/3 cup pineapple juice
2 1/2 cups instant brown rice
1/3 cup raisins
2 tablespoons ground turmeric
1 teaspoon ground cumin
1 tablespoon vegetable oil
1 onion, chopped
1 zucchini, chopped
1/2 cup chopped fresh mushrooms
1/2 red bell pepper, chopped
1/2 yellow bell pepper, chopped
2 tablespoons honey
1 tablespoon vegetable oil
1/4 cup lemon juice
1 teaspoon minced fresh ginger root
1 pinch ground black pepper
1/2 fresh pineapple - peeled, cored and chopped

<u>Directions</u>
Pour the vegetable broth, chicken broth, and pineapple juice into a large saucepan, and bring to a boil over high heat. Stir in the brown rice, raisins, turmeric, and cumin, bring back to a boil. Reduce heat to medium-low, cover, and simmer until the rice is tender, and the liquid has been absorbed, about 10 minutes. Heat 1

tablespoon of oil in a skillet over medium heat; cook and stir the onion, zucchini, mushrooms, red and yellow pepper for about 5 minutes, until the vegetables have softened. While the vegetables are cooking, stir together honey, 1 tablespoon of oil, lemon juice, ginger, and black pepper in a bowl. Stir honey mixture, cooked vegetables, and pineapple into the cooked rice, bring the mixture back to a boil, and serve hot.

Mighty Delish Moroccan Chicken

Ingredients
1 pound skinless, boneless chicken breast meat – cubed
2 teaspoons salt
1 onion, chopped
2 cloves garlic, chopped
2 carrots, sliced
2 stalks celery, sliced
1 tablespoon minced fresh ginger root
1/2 teaspoon paprika
3/4 teaspoon ground cumin
1/2 teaspoon dried oregano
1/4 teaspoon ground cayenne pepper
1/4 teaspoon ground turmeric
1 1/2 cups chicken broth
1 cup crushed tomatoes
1 cup canned chickpeas, drained
1 zucchini, sliced
1 tablespoon lemon juice
Directions

Season chicken with salt and brown in a large saucepan over medium heat until almost cooked through. Remove chicken from pan and set aside. Sauté onion, garlic, carrots and celery in same pan. When tender, stir in ginger, paprika, cumin, oregano, cayenne pepper and turmeric; stir fry for about 1 minute, then mix in broth and tomatoes Return chicken to pan, reduce heat to low and simmer for about 10 minutes. Add chickpeas and zucchini to pan and bring to simmering once again; cover pan and cook for about 15 minutes, or until zucchini is cooked through and tender. Stir in lemon juice and serve.

Mouthwatering Meatless Lasagna

Ingredients
9 uncooked lasagna noodles
1/2 cup chopped onion
2 garlic cloves, minced
2 cups diced zucchini
1 1/2 cups sliced fresh mushrooms
1 cup thinly sliced carrots
1/2 cup diced green pepper
1/2 cup diced sweet red pepper
1 (28 ounce) can crushed tomatoes
1 1/2 cups water
1 (6 ounce) can tomato paste
1 teaspoon sugar
1 teaspoon dried basil
1/2 teaspoon salt
1/2 teaspoon dried rosemary, crushed
1/4 teaspoon pepper

1 (15 ounce) container reduced-fat ricotta cheese
1 1/2 cups shredded part-skim mozzarella cheese, divided
1/4 cup grated Romano cheese

Directions

Cook lasagna noodles according to package directions. Meanwhile, in a large saucepan coated with nonstick cooking spray, sauté onion and garlic for 3 minutes. Add the zucchini, mushrooms, carrots and peppers; cook and stir until tender, about 5 minutes. Stir in the tomatoes, water, tomato paste and seasonings. Bring to a boil. reduce heat; cover and simmer for 20 minutes. Remove 2 cups sauce and set aside. Drain noodles; set aside. Combine the ricotta, 1 cup mozzarella and Romano cheese. In an ungreased 13-in. x 9-in. x 2-in. baking dish, layer a third of the remaining sauce, three noodles and half of the cheese mixture. Repeat layers. Top with remaining sauce and noodles. Spread reserved sauce over top. Cover and bake at 350 degrees F for 45 minutes. Uncover; sprinkle with remaining mozzarella. Bake 5-10 minutes longer or until cheese is melted. Let stand for 15 minutes before cutting.

Over The Rainbow Veggie Chili

<u>Ingredients</u>

2 tablespoons olive oil
1 zucchini, sliced
1 yellow squash, sliced
1 red bell pepper, diced
1 green bell pepper, diced
1 fresh jalapeno pepper, diced
4 cloves garlic, minced
1 onion, chopped
1 (28 ounce) can crushed tomatoes, with liquid
1 (6 ounce) can tomato paste
1 (15 ounce) can black beans, drained and rinsed
1 (15 ounce) can whole kernel corn, drained
1 (15 ounce) can chili beans in spicy sauce, undrained
1 tablespoon chili powder
1/2 teaspoon dried oregano
1/2 teaspoon ground black Pepper
1/4 teaspoon cayenne pepper, to taste

<u>Directions</u>

Heat oil in a large pot over medium-high heat. Stir in zucchini, yellow squash, red bell pepper, green bell pepper, jalapeno, garlic, and onion. Cook 5 minutes, just until tender. Mix tomatoes with liquid, tomato paste, black beans, corn, and chili beans in spicy sauce into the pot. Season with chili powder, oregano, black pepper, and cayenne pepper. Bring to a boil. Reduce heat to low and simmer 1 hour, stirring occasionally.

Presidential Pistou Soup

Ingredients

3 quarts vegetable broth

2 cups water

2 cups fresh green beans - rinsed, trimmed, and snapped into bite- size pieces 4 zucchini, cut into small cubes

3 carrots, cut into bite size pieces

4 potatoes, cut into bite sized pieces

1 bunch basil, leaves picked from stems

10 cloves garlic, minced

3 tomatoes, chopped

1/2 cup olive oil

1 teaspoon salt

1 (15 ounce) can kidney beans, drained and rinsed

1 (15.5 ounce) can white beans, drained and rinsed

1 (14.5 ounce) can diced tomatoes

1 (8 ounce) package spaghetti, broken into 2-inch pieces

1/2 cup shredded Gruyere cheese

1/2 cup grated Parmesan cheese

Directions

Bring the vegetable broth and water to a boil in a large pot. Stir in the green beans, zucchini, carrots, and potatoes. Return to a boil, reduce heat to medium-low, and simmer 45 minutes. Meanwhile, prepare the pistou by processing the basil leaves, garlic, tomatoes, olive oil, and salt together in a food processor until finely chopped; set aside. Stir the kidney beans, white beans, canned diced tomatoes, and spaghetti into the soup and return to a simmer. Cook until the spaghetti is tender, about 10 minutes. Remove the soup from the heat and stir in the pistou. Sprinkle with Gruyere cheese and Parmesan cheese to serve.

Prosciutto-Wrapped Chicken with Mediterranean Veggies

<u>Ingredients</u>
1/2-pound baby red potatoes, cut in half
1 zucchini, halved lengthwise and cut into 1 inch slices
1 red onion, cut into 1/2-inch thick wedges
2 red bell peppers, cut into 1 inch pieces
12 cherry tomatoes
2 tablespoons minced garlic
1/2 teaspoon dried thyme leaves
1/4 teaspoon crushed red pepper flakes
Salt and freshly ground pepper to taste
2 tablespoons olive oil
2 (5 ounce) skinless, boneless chicken breast halves
4 (1/2 ounce) slices thinly sliced prosciutto

<u>Directions</u>
Preheat oven to 400 degrees F (200 degrees C). Place potatoes, zucchini, onion, bell peppers, and tomatoes into a large bowl. Add the garlic, thyme, and red pepper flakes; season to taste with salt and pepper. Pour in olive oil, then toss until the vegetables are evenly coated with oil. Pour into a glass baking dish, and bake in preheated oven for 15 minutes. Meanwhile, season the chicken to taste with salt and pepper. Wrap each chicken breast with two slices of prosciutto, and secure with toothpicks. After the

vegetables have cooked for 15 minutes, place the prosciutto-wrapped chicken on top of the vegetables, and continue baking until the chicken has firmed and turned opaque, about 30 minutes. To serve, remove the chicken from the baking dish, and allow to rest for 5 minutes. Divide the roasted vegetables among two dinner plates. Remove toothpicks from chicken, then slice each piece of chicken into five diagonal slices. Fan the chicken out on top of the vegetables.

Rice with Summer Squash

Ingredients
1 cup chopped carrots
1/2 cup chopped onion
1 tablespoon butter
1 cup reduced sodium chicken broth or vegetable broth
1/3 cup uncooked long grain rice
1/4 teaspoon salt
1/4 teaspoon pepper
1 medium yellow summer squash, chopped
1 medium zucchini, chopped

Directions
In a saucepan coated with nonstick cooking spray, cook carrots and onion in butter until tender. Stir in the broth, rice, salt and pepper. Bring to a boil. Reduce heat; cover and simmer for 13 minutes. Stir in the yellow squash and zucchini. Cover and simmer 6-10 minutes longer or until rice and vegetables are tender.

Saucy Beef and Vegetable Casserole

Ingredients

1-pound ground beef
1 cup shredded zucchini
1 small onion, chopped
1 clove garlic, minced
1/2 teaspoon dried marjoram
1/2 cup salsa
1 (10.75 ounce) can condensed tomato soup
1 (15 ounce) can whole kernel corn, drained
1 teaspoon salt
2 cups all-purpose flour
1 tablespoon baking powder
2 teaspoons white sugar
1/2 teaspoon cream of tartar
1/2 teaspoon salt
1/8 teaspoon garlic powder
1/2 cup butter
1/2 cup shredded Cheddar cheese
1/2 cup sour cream
1 cup milk

Directions

Preheat oven to 375 degrees F (190 degrees C). Lightly grease a 9x13 inch baking dish. In a large skillet over medium heat, brown the ground beef. Drain the beef, and mix in the zucchini, onion, garlic, and marjoram. Cook and stir until vegetables are tender. Mix in the salsa, tomato soup, and corn. Season with 1 teaspoon salt. Transfer to the prepared baking dish. In a medium bowl, mix the flour, baking powder, sugar, cream of tartar, 1/2 teaspoon salt, and garlic powder.

Cut in the butter until the mixture resembles coarse crumbs. Stir in the Cheddar cheese, sour cream, and milk. Spread over the beef mixture in the baking dish. Bake covered in the preheated oven 25 minutes, or until the topping is golden brown and a toothpick inserted in the center comes out clean.

Sesame Zucchini Bread

Ingredients
3/4 cup buttermilk
1/2 cup sugar
1/2 cup packed brown sugar
1 egg white
2 tablespoons vegetable oil
2 teaspoons maple flavoring
1 1/2 cups all-purpose flour
1/2 cup whole wheat flour
1/4 cup toasted wheat germ
1 teaspoon baking powder
1 teaspoon baking soda
1/4 teaspoon salt
1/2 cup raisins
1/4 cup chopped walnuts
4 teaspoons sesame seeds, divided
1 1/2 cups shredded zucchini

Directions
In a mixing bowl, combine the first seven ingredients; beat until smooth. In another bowl, combine the flours, wheat germ, baking powder, baking soda and salt. Add raisins, walnuts and 3 teaspoons sesame seeds. Stir into sugar mixture just until moistened.

Stir in zucchini. Pour into a greased 9-in. x 5-in. x 3-in loaf pan. Sprinkle with the remaining sesame seeds. Bake at 350 degrees F for 55-60 minutes or until a toothpick inserted near the center comes out clean. Cool for 10 minute before removing from pan to a wire rack.

Spring Vegetable Medley

<u>Ingredients</u>
2 cups quartered small red potatoes
1 cup fresh baby carrots
1/2 cup water
1/2 teaspoon chicken bouillon granules
2 cups cut fresh asparagus (2 inch pieces)
1 medium zucchini, cut into 1/4- inch slices
1 tablespoon butter or margarine, melted
1 1/2 teaspoons Dijon mustard
1/2 teaspoon dried thyme
1/4 teaspoon salt

<u>Directions</u>
In a large saucepan, bring the potatoes, carrots, water and bouillon to a boil. Reduce heat; cover and simmer for 10 minutes. Add the asparagus and zucchini; cover and simmer for 10 minutes or until crisp-tender. Combine the butter, mustard, thyme and salt; pour over vegetables and toss to coat.

Stuffed Peppers with Turkey & Vegetables

Ingredients

4 green bell peppers, tops removed, seeded
1-pound ground turkey
2 tablespoons olive oil
1/2 onion, chopped
1 cup sliced mushrooms
1 zucchini, chopped
1/2 red bell pepper, chopped
1/2 yellow bell pepper, chopped
1 cup fresh spinach
1 (14.5 ounce) can diced tomatoes, drained
1 tablespoon tomato paste
Italian seasoning to taste
garlic powder to taste
salt and pepper to taste

Directions

Preheat oven to 350 degrees F (175 degrees C). Wrap the green bell peppers in aluminum foil, and place in a baking dish. Bake 15 minutes in the preheated oven. Remove from heat. In a skillet over medium heat, cook the turkey until evenly brown. Set aside. Heat oil in the skillet, and cook onion, mushrooms, zucchini, red bell pepper, yellow bell pepper, and spinach until tender. Return turkey to the skillet. Mix in the tomatoes and tomato paste, and season with Italian seasoning, garlic powder, salt, and pepper. Stuff the green peppers with the skillet mixture. Return peppers to the oven, and continue cooking 15 minutes.

Summer Bliss Veggie Casserole

Ingredients

1/4 cup olive oil
3 small zucchinis, cut in half lengthwise then into 1/4-inch slices
3 small yellow squash, cut in half lengthwise then into 1/4-inch slices
2 green bell peppers, cut into bite- size strips
2 red bell peppers, cut into bite- size strips
3 banana (or hot) peppers, seeded and chopped
2 sweet onions, sliced
5 eggs
1 cup heavy cream
2 tablespoons all-purpose flour
8 ounces processed cheese food (ex. Velveeta), cubed
2 cups seasoned bread crumbs
1 cup grated Parmesan cheese
Garlic powder to taste (optional)
Onion powder to taste (optional)
Seasoned salt to taste (optional)
Black pepper to taste (optional)

Directions

Pre-heat oven to 350 degrees F (190 degrees C). Heat olive oil in a large skillet over medium high heat. Add zucchini, yellow squash, green and red bell pepper, and onions; cook, stirring occasionally until slightly softened. Meanwhile, in a bowl, whisk together eggs, cream, and flour. When vegetables are tender, drain skillet of excess liquid and arrange in the bottom of a large glass baking dish. Season as desired with seasonings of choice, and stir to blend flavors.

Distribute cheese cubes evenly over the vegetables. Pour in the egg mixture, and spread bread crumbs and Parmesan cheese over the top. Bake in the preheated oven for 45 minutes to 1 hour, or until bubbling hot. Remove cover during the last 15 minutes to brown top lightly. Serve immediately.

Super Summer Garden Pork Chops

Ingredients
2 teaspoons salt
2 teaspoons garlic powder
2 teaspoons fresh rosemary
4 pork chops
2 carrots, chopped
1 onion, chopped
1 green bell pepper, chopped
2 leeks, chopped
1 large zucchini, chopped
2 tablespoons minced garlic
5 small tomatoes, coarsely chopped
1 cup vegetable broth
1 cinnamon stick
1/2 teaspoon ground allspice
1/3 cup olive oil
4 fresh basil leaves

Directions

Grind together salt, garlic powder and rosemary; rub onto chop. In a skillet, lightly brown in as little oil as possible; set aside. Sauté carrots, onion, green pepper, leeks, zucchini and garlic. Stir very little until they begin to caramelize or burn slightly. Layer half the vegetable mixture, including the tomatoes, in the bottom of a Dutch oven or large saucepan. Arrange the chops on top and then pour the rest of the vegetable mixture on top. Heat the vegetable stock in the sauté pan and stir to loosen bits of food on the bottom. Pour over the vegetable and pork chops. Add cinnamon stick, allspice, olive oil and basil. Simmer for 20 minutes.

Vegetarian Lasagna

<u>Ingredients</u>
1 (16 ounce) can diced tomatoes
1 (16 ounce) package instant lasagna noodles
1 bunch fresh spinach, washed and chopped
2 large carrots, shredded
2 large zucchinis, diced
2 summer squash, diced
1 large eggplant, diced
1 large head broccoli, cut into florets
2 teaspoons dried oregano
salt and pepper to taste
1 cup shredded mozzarella cheese (optional)
1 cup ricotta cheese (optional)
<u>Directions</u>
Preheat oven to 375 degrees F (190 degrees C). Lightly grease one 9x13 inch baking dish. Place a layer of tomatoes in the bottom of the baking dish, followed by a layer of noodles, spinach, carrots, zucchini, summer squash, eggplant and broccoli. Season to taste with oregano, salt and pepper. Repeat layering of <u>Ingredients</u> until all are used up. If using cheeses

sprinkle over broccoli layers and on top of dish. Bake at 375 degrees F (190 degrees C) for 25 to 35 minutes.

Veggie Shrimp Fettuccine

Ingredients

4 ounces uncooked fettuccine
1 medium onion, chopped
1 medium zucchini, cut into 1/4- inch slices
1 medium tomato, seeded and chopped
1 garlic clove, minced
2 tablespoons butter
1/2-pound uncooked medium shrimp, peeled and deveined
2 tablespoons white wine or chicken broth
1/4 teaspoon salt
1/8 teaspoon pepper

Directions

Cook fettuccine according to package directions. Meanwhile, in a skillet, sauté the onion, zucchini, tomato and garlic in butter for 8-10 minutes or until crisp-tender. Add the shrimp, wine or broth, salt and pepper. Cook 3-4 minutes longer or until shrimp turn pink. Drain fettuccine; top with shrimp mixture.

Veggie Stir-Fry

Ingredients

2 teaspoons cornstarch
1/2 cup cold water
3 tablespoons soy sauce
1 cup fresh broccoli florets
1 medium carrot, thinly sliced

1/2 small onion, julienned
1 tablespoon vegetable oil
1 cup shredded cabbage
1 small zucchini, julienned
6 large mushrooms, sliced
1/2 teaspoon minced garlic
Hot cooked rice

Directions

In a small bowl, whisk the cornstarch, water and soy sauce until smooth; set aside. In a large skillet or wok, stir-fry the broccoli, carrot and onion in oil for 5 minutes. Add the cabbage, zucchini, mushrooms and garlic. Stir-fry until vegetables are tender. Stir soy sauce mixture; add to skillet. Cook and stir until thickened. Serve with rice if desired.

Zesty Zucchini with Salsa

Ingredients

1 medium onion, diced
1 tablespoon minced fresh cilantro
2 garlic cloves, minced
2 jalapeno peppers, seeded and minced (optional)
3 green onions, sliced
3 medium tomatoes, diced
4 medium zucchini, sliced
Salt and pepper to taste

Directions

Divide zucchini between two pieces of heavy-duty foil (about 20 in. x 18 in.). In a bowl, combine the remaining ingredients; spoon over zucchini. Fold foil around vegetables and seal tightly. Grill, covered, over indirect heat for 15-20 minutes or until vegetables are tender.

Zucchilattas

Ingredients

2 tablespoons butter
1 1/2 pounds sliced zucchini
1 pound mushrooms, sliced
1 onion, sliced
1 1/2 pounds tomatoes, chopped
Salt and pepper to taste
1 1/2 pounds Monterey Jack cheese, shredded
10 (10 inch) flour tortillas

Directions

Preheat oven to 350 degrees F (175 degrees C). Lightly grease a 9x13 inch baking dish. Melt butter in a large skillet over medium heat. Mix together the zucchini, mushrooms, onion, tomatoes, salt and pepper, and add to the skillet. Cook and stir until the vegetables are soft. Warm the tortillas 2 to 3 minutes, until soft, in the preheated oven. Fill the warmed tortillas with zucchini mixture and Monterey Jack cheese, reserving some of both for toppings. Roll the filled tortillas and place them seam side down in the baking dish. Cover with the remaining zucchini mixture. Top with remaining cheese. Bake in the preheated oven 15 minutes, or until the cheese is bubbly.

Zucchini Cobbler

<u>Ingredients</u>

8 cups peeled, chopped zucchini
2/3 cup lemon juice
1 cup white sugar
1 teaspoon ground cinnamon
1/2 teaspoon ground nutmeg
4 cups all-purpose flour
2 cups white sugar
1 1/2 cups butter, chilled
1 teaspoon ground cinnamon

<u>Directions</u>

In a large saucepan over medium heat, cook and stir zucchini and lemon juice until zucchini is tender, 15 to 20 minutes. Stir in 1 cup sugar, 1 teaspoon cinnamon and nutmeg and cook one minute more. Remove from heat and set aside. Preheat oven to 375 degrees F (190 degrees C). Grease a 10x15 inch baking dish. In a large bowl, combine flour and 2 cups sugar. Cut in butter with pastry blender or two knives until mixture resembles coarse crumbs. Stir 1/2 cup of butter mixture into zucchini mixture. Press half of remaining butter mixture into bottom of prepared pan. Spread zucchini mixture over top of crust, and sprinkle remaining butter mixture over zucchini. Sprinkle with 1 teaspoon cinnamon. Bake 35 to 40 minutes, or until top is golden. Serve warm or cold.

Zucchini Cocoa Cupcakes

Ingredients

2 (1 ounce) squares unsweetened chocolate, melted
3 eggs
1 3/4 cups packed brown sugar
1 cup vegetable oil
2 cups all-purpose flour
1 teaspoon baking powder
1 teaspoon baking soda
1/2 teaspoon salt
2 cups grated zucchini
3/4 cup chopped walnuts
1 (16 ounce) package chocolate frosting
1/2 cup walnut halves

Directions

Preheat the oven to 350 degrees F (175 degrees C). In a large bowl, beat eggs with sugar for about 10 minutes or until thickened and pale. Blend oil and cooled chocolate into the beaten egg mixture. In a small bowl stir together flour, baking powder, baking soda and salt; stir flour mixture into egg mixture until just blended. Stir in zucchini and chopped nuts. Using an ice-cream scoop, spoon batter into 24 paper-lined or greased muffin cups, filling the cups 2/3 full. Bake for 20 minutes or until fork or toothpick inserted in a cupcake's center comes out clean. Let cool in pans on rack for 10 minutes. Remove from pans; let cool completely. Spread with chocolate frosting and garnish with walnut or pecan halves.

Zucchini Cream Pie

Ingredients

1 1/2 cups zucchini - peeled, seeded and sliced
1 cup evaporated milk
2 cups white sugar
3 tablespoons margarine
3 tablespoons all-purpose flour
1 teaspoon vanilla extract
1 pinch salt
1 9 inch, unbaked single crust pie
1/2 teaspoon ground cinnamon
1/4 teaspoon ground nutmeg

Directions

Boil zucchini until tender. Drain and let stand in cold water for about 5 minutes, then drain. Put the zucchini, evaporated milk, sugar, egg, margarine, flour, vanilla and salt into a blender and blend until smooth. Pour into unbaked pie shell. Sprinkle with cinnamon and nutmeg. Bake at 425 degrees F (220 degrees C) for 5 minutes. Reduce heat to 325 degrees F (165 degrees C) and bake until set.

Zucchini Pineapple Bread

Ingredients

3 eggs, beaten
2 cups white sugar
1 teaspoon vanilla extract
1 cup vegetable oil
2 cups grated zucchini
3 cups all-purpose flour
1 teaspoon baking soda
1 teaspoon baking powder
1 teaspoon salt
1/2 cup raisins
1 cup chopped pecans
1 cup crushed pineapple, drained

Directions

In a large bowl mix together the eggs, sugar, vanilla, oil and zucchini. In a separate bowl mix together the flour, soda, baking powder, and salt. Add to the zucchini batter and mix well. Stir in raisins, nuts, and pineapple until just blended. Pour into 2-9x5x3 inch loaf pans. Bake in a preheated 325-degree F (165 degrees C) for one hour, or until browned.

Zucchini Walnut Bread

<u>Ingredients</u>

1 cup chopped walnuts
4 eggs
2 cups white sugar
1 cup vegetable oil
3 1/2 cups all-purpose flour
1 1/2 teaspoons baking soda
1 1/2 teaspoons salt
1 teaspoon ground cinnamon
3/4 teaspoon baking powder
2 cups grated zucchini
1 cup raisins
1 teaspoon vanilla extract

<u>Directions</u>

Whisk together flour, baking soda, salt, cinnamon, and baking powder. In a large bowl, beat the eggs. Gradually beat in sugar, then oil. Add flour mixture alternately with zucchini into the egg mixture. Stir in the raisins, walnuts, and vanilla. Pour batter into two 9 x 5 inch greased and lightly floured loaf pans. Bake on lowest rack of the oven at 350 degrees F (175 degrees C) for 55 minutes. Let cool for 10 minutes in the pan, then turn out onto racks to cool completely. To freeze, wrap loaves in plastic wrap, and then wrap in heavy freezer paper. Will keep indefinitely.

Zucchini-Coconut Cookie Bars

<u>Ingredients</u>

3/4 cup margarine, softened
1/2 cup white sugar
1/2 cup packed brown sugar
2 eggs
1 teaspoon vanilla extract
1 3/4 cups all-purpose flour
1/2 teaspoon salt
1 1/2 teaspoons baking powder
3/4 cup flaked coconut
3/4 cup chopped pitted dates
3/4 cup raisins
2 cups grated zucchini
1 tablespoon margarine, melted
2 tablespoons milk
1 teaspoon vanilla extract
1/4 teaspoon ground cinnamon
1 cup confectioners' sugar
1 cup finely chopped walnuts

<u>Directions</u>

Preheat oven to 350 degrees F (175 degrees C). Grease a 9x13 inch baking pan. In a large bowl, cream together the butter, white sugar, and brown sugar. Mix in eggs and 1 teaspoon vanilla until fluffy. Sift together the flour, salt, and baking powder; stir into the creamed mixture. Stir in the coconut, dates, raisins, and zucchini. Spread batter into the prepared pan. Bake in preheated oven for 35 to 40 minutes. To make icing, mix together melted margarine, milk, 1 teaspoon vanilla, cinnamon, and confectioners' sugar. Drizzle icing over the bars while still warm. Sprinkle chopped nuts over icing. Cut into bars when cool.

Zucchini-Potato Soup

Ingredients

5 cups chicken broth
4 small zucchinis, thinly sliced
1 large potato, peeled, halved and thinly sliced
1 large onion, thinly sliced
3 eggs
2 tablespoons lemon juice
2 teaspoons dried dill weed
salt and pepper to taste

Directions

In a saucepan, bring broth to a boil. Stir in zucchini, potato and onion. Reduce heat and simmer, covered, 15 minutes or until vegetables are tender. In a small bowl, beat eggs; blend in lemon juice and 1/2 cup hot broth. Stir back into the saucepan. Heat over medium for 1 minute, stirring constantly. D0 not boil. Stir in dill; season with salt and pepper. Serve immediately.

****

Thanks for your purchase!
♥♥♥♥♥♥

Find more Dahlia Orion cookbooks at
https://amzn.to/2ZQiozC.

Made in United States
North Haven, CT
03 July 2025